# From the Heart of a Poet

*Straight from the Heart*

*Genie Simmons*

PRESS

# *Dedications*

*My dear friend*
*Carolyn Harris*
*and*
*In memory of my late parents*
*Elder Ernest G. Simmons and Carnell Cousar Simmons*
*Mike A. Gomez - first crush*

# *Acknowledgements*

*First and foremost I would like to thank my Lord and Savior Jesus Christ who is the author and finisher of my faith, for the ability of expression in words and how to put them together, not only in this book but also in song, plays and novels.*

*Carolyn Harris, a former employee at the V-8 Engine Plant in Flint, Michigan. My sister in Jesus Christ. I Thank You for your encouragement in my ability to write this book, <u>From The Heart Of A Poet</u>.*

*To my former co-workers at the V-8 Engine Plant in Flint, Michigan. Thank You for your suggestions in subject matters to write about. Thank you Brenda, Charles and Miranda. Thank you Doris, Frieda, Annie, Alma and Bonnie, for being the listening ear and a good sounding board.*

*To my four babies, who will always be that to me: Levi, Gregory, Roslyn, and Jennifer. You were there for me; you heard it all and all. Thanks for listening to your Mama, her songs, her stories and her poems.*

*Mother Lillian Dunlap, Thank You. For without your broadcast and the selling of your book <u>Go to Sleep With Mother's Prayers</u>, Carolyn would not have conceived the idea that I should write a book of poetry and I would not have given it a thought.*

*Mrs. Juanita Meares of Fayetteville, North Carolina, my oldest sister for reading all my books and for your encouragement. I love you for all the years you were there for me.*

*Thank you Sue, Connie and Rose from the Learning Center at the Romulus GM PowerTrain Plant. You are "The Greatest" and "Thank You" for also being my proofreaders and my friends. My friend Rose who stayed behind until I finished the rewrites, I love you.*

*The late Elder Ernest G. Simmons, Sr. who exposed me to the world of Literature and Fine Arts. My mentor, my friend and my Daddy, I miss you.*

*My mother, the late Carnell Cousar Simmons, who loved and believed in me and wanted the best for me, who also told me that God had great things in my life yet to perform. Maybe this is just one of them "mom."*

*My beloved twin sister Jeanette, who never had the chance to share a long life with me, or witness the talents that God had bestowed on me, and for whom the poem, Twins was written.*

*Finally to Bishop T.D. Jakes for your words of wisdom in your book Maximize The Moment, as well as knowing My Season.*

# Table of Contents

## Inspirational

## Other Issues

*Facets of Life*
*Life is full of ups and downs*

# *Abandon*

*Hey! Are you my Dad*
*You look just like him*
*My mother told me, don't be sad*
*He is a poor excuse for a Dad*
*If I really knew him, it would make me mad*
*I saw him once or twice in my life*
*Then he was gone from sight*
*I was young when this begun*
*He thought being a Dad would be fun*
*Oh! I would see him a little bit at times*
*I suppose I wasn't on his mind*
*Ignoring me must have been easy*
*My Dad gave me up so freely*
*I am older now and there's distance between us*
*I understand a little better now, why he and mom would fuss*
*She is your child, you haven't seen her in a while*
*You expect a little too much*
*From her there is resentment as such*
*When a father refuses to be a good Dad*
*What can you expect but your child to be sad*

*For Brenda Goodman*

## *A Bride*

*Looking into the mirror at the reflection that I see*
*I have become a Bride to be*
*In the next few minutes my life will change*
*I am committing to be his wife for the rest of my life*
*Promises that we are about to take*
*In sickness and in health as long as we both shall live*
*To each other our love we will freely give*
*For better or worse, for richer or poor*
*I know I could not love you more*
*My life I committed to God a long time ago*
*So his laws and commandments I know*
*Husband love your wife as Christ loves the church*
*Then I know our marriage will work*
*This man is now my husband and I his wife*
*It will be for the rest of our life*

# A Dieter's Nightmare

*Who me? I've never had a problem with my weight*
*Cookies, candies mostly junk food I ate*
*From Burger King, KFC to Mickey D's*
*Never thought the person I see would be me*
*Now I'm looking at myself and hoping it's not too late*
*Wish I could say, it's not me, so it must be a mistake*

*There are all kinds of bad habits, I will agree*
*It seems that eating is the one for me*
*However like some smokers, it's hard to quit*
*If asked they would admit*
*The things they have tried*
*Nevertheless, pounds you just can't hide*
*Just keep telling yourself you know what to do*
*Eating healthier is better for you*

*If you are serious about the weight you want to lose*
*You have to make up your mind…you have to choose*
*You have tried eating small amounts before*
*Found it hard and such a chore*
*The diets you tried were all a fad*
*Eating junk food made you glad*

*Now it's amazing when you get past the age of forty*
*You realize what has happened that's when you cry O'Lordy*
*Now the weight has remained*
*Except there is twenty more pounds you've gained*
*Decision you make to lose this weight*
*Only becomes more when you hesitate*

# *Can We Ever Go Home Again*

*It's raining and it's cold*
*I see young people and old*
*Who want to go home again*
*There's no place to rest their tired head*
*Or to cover up in a nice warm bed*
*They just want to go home again*

*Sleeping in city streets*
*There are times there is no food to eat*
*Sleeping in an abandon car or a bus*
*Lord what is to happen to us*
*In an alley or on a bench in the park*
*It's all scary when it's dark*
*It was a twist of fate that they couldn't escape*
*Things can change it's never too late*
*When the sun shines it give us a ray of hope*
*Each day we survive for we have learned how to cope*
*But can we ever go home again*
*Inspired by photos in the Flint Journal*

# *Colors*

*I never saw colors*
*Only in a rainbow I didn't know*
*I was young and naïve I wasn't raised that way*
*Things can be different from yesterday*
*The hatred, the violence and mistrust*
*What is the difference in us*
*You see me, not what I can be*

*I am older now*
*I still see only the colors in the rainbow*
*How they flow together*
*The red, yellow, green and blue*
*There are other colors too*
*Why can't a world filled with colors*
*Know that same flow*

*What a thing to see*
*When we can live in harmony*
*Look past my color*
*Only see me as your brother*
*When we can get past what we see*
*Then you and I are free*
*Imagine a world where there is peace*
*All because hatred has ceased*
*That would be such a relief*
*To know this color thing doesn't have to be*

# It's A Reality

It's a reality that nothing is the same
Some have losses others have gains
Job security is a thing of the past
With layoffs who knew this would last
With department stores and plants closing too
Take a guess to what is going to happen I don't have a clue

It's a reality that things in life do change
Our view of it may not be the same
As in life we embrace
Like death, we don't want to face
Divorce is on the rise
Children in the middle having to choose sides
There are murders, abortions and even suicides
Drugs, robberies even companies polluting the skies
Now it makes you ask the question why

Now let's not forget how the fashions change
From up to down, short or long
A new season of styles and then it's gone
Long hair, to no hair
It was up to you what you wanted to wear
Weave or braids a color or tint
Whatever your flair that's the way it went
It's a reality that things in life change
It's been here before yet different but the same

# *Once Upon A Princess*

*She was only nineteen*
*Someday she would have been the Queen*
*She was compassionate toward mankind*
*Any faults others had she was blind to*
*She grew to be a fine regal of a lady*
*She was also the mother of two babies*
*She had a good heart big as the sea*
*Her private life the "press" wouldn't let it be*

*There are many things I could say*
*However, I will sum it up this way*
*I, like many other little girls*
*Wished for a Prince Charming*
*There may be things about him that could be very alarming*
*Like Snow White, she was gentle and sweet*
*To everyone she would meet*
*Like Cinderella, she thought the man she married*
*Was the right fella*

*Grace and style our Princess had*
*Now millions of people are shocked and sad*
*Of a Princess who is laid to rest*
*A Princess who only gave her best*
*She was called a People Princess*
*Who will be sadly missed*
*Was that Prince a frog she kissed*

*Little girls everywhere, be careful for what you wish*
*It might be a frog that you kiss*
*Only in fairytales is a Prince a Prince*
*Never before nor since*
*She will never grace our doors*
*She will be alive in our memories forevermore*

**A salute to**
**The Late Princess of Wales**
**Diana**

# *Single Again*

*Some say you were too young to be a bride*
*Who knew the man you married would make you cry*
*A broken heart he left you with*
*When he threw up his hands and called it quits*
*Here you are after so many years*
*Being single is one of your fears*
*Yet, here you are again*
*Thankful for the support from your friends*
*Only difference now you are not alone as before*
*You have the custody of four*

*The responsibility of the house and more*
*All because he walked out the door*
*It's not easy with the bills and no time for yourself*
*Your life has to be put on a shelf*
*The needs of your children come first*
*Sometimes a quiet moment is all you thirst*
*Oh! Getting back into the dating game has change*
*It's certainly not the same*
*It isn't as easy as it seems*
*For so many years, you were a team*

*Nevertheless, here you are single once again*
*With a little encouragement from your friends*
*Reminding you there is life after divorce*
*As if you had a choice*
*You are strong and you will survive*
*For each day you take it in stride*
*When you are ready for romance in your life*
*You will consider everything even the price*

# *Taking A Wife*

*This is the day, when you become my wife*
*I will love and cherish you all my life*
*As I stand before God and Man*
*I look into your eyes, and I'll take your hand*
*To be joined together*
*No one but you on this day matters*
*United as one of the same mind, body and soul*
*Building a life together is my ultimate goal*
*Because with you I am made whole*
*My partner for life everything for you I'll do right*
*I know you will follow me in all I do*
*To make this relationship last through time*
*Because I'm yours and you are mine*
*Each step I make, we make as one*
*Your pain is my pain*
*Your joy is my joy*
*I am in sync with you, cause you are my life*
*Today you became my wife*

**Charles & Carla Collins**
**September 2000**

## *The Teacher's Pet*

*What makes her so special*
*I asked myself why*
*She chose you and not I*
*I've seen the things that she does just for you*
*It's not a secret, for others have seen it too*
*This I won't ever forget*
*Just how much I wanted to be*
*The Teacher's Pet*

# The Children Are Crying

*Parents are confused*
*While their children are being abused*
*Does anybody care, is anybody aware*
*Of their suffering and their pain*
*In addition to the scars that remain*
*Children missing from their homes*
*Nobody knows where they have gone*
*THE CHILDREN ARE CRYING*

*What can we do to ease their pain*
*When so many scars remain*
*And a parent's guilt or their shame*
*Agencies that know what to do*
*So there is help for your child and you*

*These are our children of tomorrow*
*Oh what sadness Dear God, what sorrow*
*The children are crying, while others are dying*
*Children missing from their homes*
*No one knows how long they will be gone*
*Does anybody care. Yes! The world is finally aware*

# *Today's Society*

*Today's generation so mixed up and confused*
*A society in which children and old are being abused*
*People wake up! It's time for a change*
*Things can be different they don't have to be the same*
*The weapons of war battle in the streets*
*Innocence is dying wrapped in blood-stained sheets*
*Elderly people who aren't safe in their homes*
*Children unattended left all alone*

*Hatred, violence, in the hearts of men*
*How in the world did this all begin*
*First prayer was taken out of the schools*
*Now the youth of today don't want to obey any rules*
*Homes where no man can be found*
*Some in the jails, others buried in the ground*
*A society where women are taking care of men*
*It used to be the other way, things have changed since then*

*Teens are pregnant some as early as fifteen*
*Things are hard so finances are lean*
*Get a job, get an education*
*It's not your only salvation*
*Hey people, wake up! It's time for a change*
*Or else, things will be the same*

# *Young Folks*

*This is not a joke*
*To poke fun of the young folks*
*Some ain't got no Manners*
*Some act as though they have gone bananas*
*Some are as smart as a whip*
*Some can't handle life cause they ain't got a grip*
*What some young folks won't do*
*They are forever surprising me and you*
*Some drop out of school mighty young*
*The things they have experienced*
*You and I ain't never done*
*They play with a gun as though it was a toy*
*They will shoot a girl so you know they will shoot a boy*
*Having babies every now and then*
*Aborting them as though it ain't no Sin!*
*Young folks ain't got no self-esteem*
*Some of them is down right mean*
*Some are as pretty as pie*
*You got some, look ya square in the face and lie*
*I'll say it again, Prayer was taken out of the schools*
*How can you expect our young folks to obey any rules*
*The Courts told you and me not to punish our child*
*Now look at them crazy children running wild*
*Who can we blame, be honest it's a down right shame*
*These are our young folks*
*Some young folks will adjust*
*You got some young folks, you can trust*
*There are some mighty fines ones too*
*Cause the right thing they will always do*
*Not all the young folks are bad seeds*
*Our love and support is what they really need*

*In The Family*
*We have each other*

# Adoption
## (A gift of love)

Once I had laid eyes on you
I was helpless; I knew what I had to do
Therefore, I adopted this baby girl
Who filled the emptiness of my world
Fat and cuddly, cute as can be
I would hold her for everyone to see
From my lap, to my knee
I have watched you become somebody
You were my child not from my womb
But from my heart
I knew nothing would tear us apart
Now years have gone by
I am your mother and I don't understand why
I've made sacrifices to give you the best
Now you complain and you are putting my nerves to the test
Everything I have done for you was out of love
All I see is an ungrateful, selfish and greedy child
Who runs the street as though she's wild
Not much, I ask only a little respect from you
I don't think that is too hard to do
"Children obey your parents" this is what the Bible said
Lord have mercy if you don't do the opposite instead
I can't believe what brought us to this point
I am your mother
For there isn't another

**Inspired by Miranda**

# Daddy's Little Girl

*There's nothing better in the whole world*
*Than being Dad's little girl*
*My Dad was tall; some Dads are short*
*There are Dads of every sort*
*Some lean, some fat*
*Some Dads are just cool cats*
*My Dad was a man of faith*
*One day I will see him standing at Heaven's gate*
*Oh! I come from a family of six kids*
*My oldest sister was a college whiz*
*My oldest brothers were military aimed*
*Me, Daddy said, I like to play games*
*As a little girl, I was bounced on his knee*
*When his work was done for the day, it was me*
*Daddy would see*
*For he preached the gospel to everyone even me*
*Cause he didn't want me bound but free*
*He gave all he had to give*
*If wishes were granted my Dad would have lived*
*Oh! I'm not sad*
*Because if I am good and not bad*
*I'll be in Heaven, and I will be glad*
*Cause you know what, I'll be with my Dad*

# Diabetes & Me

*I thought this happened when you got old*
*I was in a state of shock when I was told*
*I'm too young is what I said*
*If you don't take care of yourself, you will be dead*
*Now this is what my doctor said*
*However I choose to live instead*
*I didn't look sick nor did I feel ill*
*So this can't be happening it can't be real*

*Now my life has changed*
*Ever since then nothing has been the same*
*Taking medication, exercising and eating right too*
*These things I now have to do*
*I call diabetes a generational curse*
*From pills to insulin because things got worse*
*I wouldn't wish this on my worst friend*
*A cure is what I need, just don't know when*
*One day at a time it will get better*
*To me that is all that matters*
*I'll do what is right*
*Just to save my life*

*Now diabetes effect many body parts*
*Even that big muscle called the heart*
*My blood pressure went from low to high*
*So I do what is necessary to live and not die*
*You see diabetes is no joke*
*It can cause a heart attack or a stroke*
*Follow simple instruction is what I must do*
*To save My own life it's up to me not you*

# *Homesick*

*I'm homesick for the country air*
*And the easy living there*
*Remembering how things use to be*
*I've had visions you see*
*After several months of dealing with the snow*
*I'm glad to see it go*
*It will be sunshine and blue skies*
*So I'm going to say my good-byes*

*Now I realize things have changed a lot*
*I have my memories so I haven't forgot*
*All you could see was miles of dirt roads*
*In addition to the tobacco that grows*
*You know life was a little slower*
*Your neighbor didn't live right next door*

*My roots are calling me home*
*Just look how long I've been gone*
*My children are all grown*
*And have lives of their own*
*Now if you miss me you know what to do*
*Drop me a line or two*
*I will be glad to hear from you*
*Now if you telephone me that would be better*
*Cause you would hear from me faster than a letter*

*There will be plenty of things for me to do*
*There is the Church, home mission*
*Oh! Just all sorts of things I will be into*
*Now don't forget I will be looking to hearing from all of you*

*If you come looking for me*
*Just remember I'll be under mama's big pecan tree*
*In my hand will be a tall glass of ice tea*
*Now it gets hot sometime*

*You can feel a breeze and hear the chime*
*You can smell the fish and hush puppies inviting*
*You to come and join us*
*These are just some of the reasons I get homesick*
*For the country air and the easy living there*

**Dedicated to Mrs. Myrtle Bell**
**My play mom**

# Honey I'm Home
## (After thirty plus years)
## Of being gone

Now that you about to turn another page in life
Look at all the time you will have to spend with your wife
Remember this, don't get on her nerves and stay out of her way
It's possible she will let you live another day
So find something else to do and the wife you love will thank you
Get out of that chair and turn the television off
Try your hand at a little game of golf
She knows you love to bowl but it's time for a change
Hey your bowling average went down so it ain't the same
Chasing young girls, now it ain't a good sport
Your heart can't take it, and your breathing is now a little short
Just forget about what you wish
Don't think about the things you have missed
Enjoy what you had yesterday cause it's gone
Your friends aren't there so you are left alone
See what happens when you stay too long

**Written for Oscar Ridley**
**Who retired 01/2001**

# *It's My Life*

*I've never ridden on a Harley, on the open wide strip*
*Finally, I'd did take a trip on the Carnival Cruise Ship*
*I've never been to Alaska in the dead winter cold*
*However, if I live a good life, I will live to get old*
*Cause it's my life*
*I've always enjoyed my life*
*Despite the fact when I am wrong, I still try to do what is right*
*I'm glad I have a relationship with Jesus Christ*
*You know I have had some worries and frets*
*It is the love and support of my family I will never forget*
*There were moments, when I didn't see my way*
*I knew what to do, so I would drop to my knees and pray*
*Even in my life, I've given romance a try*
*When things went wrong, I wondered why*
*I have been fortunate to get around*
*I have traveled to distant towns*
*I've seen some historical places*
*The countries I have visited; I met people of different races*
*When I retire then, I will rest*
*Just to reflect over the things I've done*
*I would say I lived a good life, and boy didn't I have fun*

# *I'm Retired*

*I have worked hard all my life*
*So that things would be right*
*Now that my kids are all grown*
*I can relax and enjoy my home*

*When I retired from my job*
*It wasn't to baby-sit Mary and Bob*
*Now there are things I would like to do*
*That doesn't involve any of you*
*I am not as young as I used to be*
*So, don't try to take advantage of me*

*Yes I know these are my grandchildren*
*And I love them very dearly*
*Sometimes I do get a little weary*
*I didn't retire just to be your sitter*
*And to pick up the trash that they litter*
*Oh! They are beautiful and sweet*
*But when I want to rest, they won't go to sleep*
*Now that my shift from work is done*
*I have some good years left to have some fun*

# *Mama's Gone*

*I am left here all alone*
*Now that my Mama is gone*
*The emptiness I feel inside*
*The day my Mama died*
*She told me to hold on*
*For my family, I had to be strong*
*It was hard trying to cope*
*When I couldn't see a ray of hope*
*The tears I have tried to hide*
*They reflect the pain I feel inside*
*Seems as though it was just yesterday*
*I could hear my Mama say*
*"Daughter kneel and pray*
*God will help you see your way"*
*My Mama is gone*
*Didn't she know that I would need her one day*

*Her patience a virtue, needless to say*
*Her skin smooth and fair*
*Her laughter seemed to fill the air*
*Her tender touch showed she cared*
*If there were problems Mama sure was aware*
*She never raised her voice or such*
*Mama loved her children so very much*
*She made us feel good about ourselves*
*She encouraged our growth above everything else*
*She gave us all the tools we would ever need*
*She provided the ingredients to help us succeed*
*Though my Mama died yours may be alive*
*Let her know she is a special prize*
*I have many memories of Mama*
*I know she is not gone Her spirit lingers on*
*Her presence will always be felt with me*
*That is the way I want it to be*
*Mama wanted to live to see her babies grown*
*Now that she has*
*Mama's Gone*

**A dedication to Carnell Cousar Simmons**
**My Mother**

# She's Old Enough

*Why can't she have fun, she's not old but young*
*She liked Rock-n-Roll, for the stories that they told*
*People say, "being young is a breath of fresh air*
*That the youth don't have any worries or care"*
*Have you forgot, you've been there*

*Remember the Diary of Anne Frank*
*Living in America makes you give thanks*
*Freedom of Choice, of speech*
*Freedom is what she seeks*

*Every country, city and state are governed by laws*
*She would just love to be free that's all*
*Politics she would leave to the Politicians*
*Economics to the Economists*
*She would just like to see a change*
*But it's not happening so far things are still the same*

*She has graduated from high school*
*Like anyone else she feels she has paid her dues*
*To further her education is just a dream*
*It's so far out of reach it seems*
*Marriage is a possible escape*
*It would open that gate*
*To the freedom that awaits*

*It would be a change in her life*
*It she became a wife*
*Just know she is old enough to be engaged*
*No woman wants to be an Old Maid*
*Can you imagine living in a country where you are not free*
*Where you can't come and go as you please*
*I think not believe you me!*

41

# *This Child Is Mine*

*He will be taught right from wrong*
*As I gaze upon this sleeping child*
*I notice the most beautiful smile*
*His skin smooth and fair*
*He will know that his mother cares*
*For him, she will always be there*
*For this child is mine*

*He will find strength in himself*
*Not just to gain worldly wealth*
*To have pride in the man he has become*
*All that he has learned he will pass it on to his son*
*He will respect and love the woman who has become his wife*
*For I have given him a foundation in Jesus Christ*
*He will know that in Him only can he have hope*
*Whatever happens, my son will be able to cope*
*He will survive in this life*
*For I have taught him what is right*
*Whatever happens in this span of time*
*This Child is Mine*

# *Twins*

He was there in the beginning of my life
I was too young to know it was Jesus Christ
When my life was hanging by a thread
In addition to the fact that my twin sister was already dead
He was there, and he cared
Even though, I was not aware

Some things happen for a reason
As a purpose for every season
Identical to a T
How do you know for sure it's me
There is an absence in my life
I don't know how to make it right

I see twins every now and then
They are closer than friends
One may be tall, one might be fat
They don't seem to run with a pack
These twins have each other
Even though, they have other sisters and brothers

They sometimes dress alike
Twins sometimes fight
It's like hitting yourself
A mirror image you are
For your twin you will go the distance
Doesn't matter how far
Death separated us very young
Before our lives could have begun
She is an angel that I have touched
My twin, I do miss so much

**A tribute to Jeanette Simmons**
**My Twin Sister**

# *Two Sisters*

*One day I stopped to say*
*Hello to a neighbor by the way*
*I am just an outsider looking in*
*These two girls, I thought were Friends*
*Who would have thought*
*The way these Two Sisters fought*
*I believe there is love somewhere in their hearts*
*Even though, they were born four years apart*
*You see I have seen a glimpse*
*Of their caring for one another*
*I have seen it shown with their brothers*
*I don't understand, why these two can't get along*

*I wonder what is wrong*
*Is it the age difference between them*
*Their Father, I'm acquainted with him*
*Their Mother has tried and done her best*
*Sometimes she wishes they would give it a rest*
*Are there instructions on how to behave*
*Before these Girls, drive their Mother to an early grave*
*Sometimes Sisters may disagree*
*It's in those times; it may be a turn over the knee*
*A hug or a kiss and make up*
*These sisters only pretend to be tough*
*They sometimes share, I know they care*
*I am not an outsider but a mom I am aware*
*Love sometimes is hard to show*
*So leave the situation alone and let it go*
*Who would have ever thought*
*They way these TWO SISTERS fought*

*Inspirational*
***The Lor****d is my strength*

# A Song

*A song can express what you may be feeling*
*At that moment in time*
*For its speaks exactly what is on your mind*
*It maybe a test that you just went through*
*It will be your testimony to what God can do*

*A song will bring you from down to up*
*Yes! We all have had to drink from life's bitter cup*
*There are so many songs that one can sing*
*Only the praises of God should ring*

*Remember the song*
*"It is no secret what God can do"*
*I find myself humming it too*
*It is amazing what a song will do*
*Even if you may not have heard it in a long time*
*If you listen it will be echoing in the back of your mind*

## *A Heart Full Of Melodies*

*Dear Jesus, I was troubled yesterday*
*So I dropped to my knees to pray*
*There were so many words I wanted to say*
*Besides Lord thank you for this day*
*I was so filled up*
*I remember how you had filled my cup*
*Not very much strength did I possess*
*So I took to my bed for some rest*
*As I laid there, a song came to me*
*It began to stir in my soul*
*The song began to build me up*
*With the message that it told*

*"Just a closer walk with thee*
*Grant it Jesus if you please*
*I'll be satisfied as long*
*As I walk let me walk close to thee"*

*As I began to rejoice in these words*
*I heard the voices of little girls*
*Echoing in my mind*
*It was a different day and time*
*I felt so much better*
*Minutes ago I was under the weather*
*In my heart there were melodies around me*
*Once again I began to trust what I didn't see*
*I sought a closer walk with thee*

# *Emergency*
# *(A Bad Dream)*

*Hello, Hello is anyone there*
*I'm sorry, I heard a voice say*
*Don't hang up Hey! I need help today*
*Then the voice said to me there is an interruption in the line*
*Please try your number at a later time*
*This is an emergency, I cried*
*I have to get through*
*I don't know what else to do*
*Is there anyone else there I can talk to*
*I need to be rescued from this life of eternal death*
*I'm only asking for, forgiveness and to be set free*
*I didn't really believe this is the way it would be*
*For God is a merciful God, a good Savior*
*It wasn't my intent to waiver*
*Oh Lord, why did I wait too late*
*From where I am, I can't see Heaven's gate*
*Is it really too late can anything be done*
*There is no place to hide or run*
*Heavenly Father I pray this is just a bad dream*
*Please wake me and I will let your praises ring*

# I Know It's Hard
## (The loss of a son)

I can't identify with your pain
I do understand just the same
It is hard I do know
To death I lost my parents not long ago
Let God have it, He will fix it just so
He is still God, and He is very much aware
Of your sorrow and he does care
Just remember in God you have hope
His strength in any situation to cope
It is okay to cry, for we cry with you
We don't know what else to do
We don't expect a smile
Just know that it will get better in a while

He was always on your mind
So remember the good times
Remember how you watched him grow
The things you taught him to know
Keep the memories always in your heart
That is where he lives so you are never apart
Remember the scraped knees
The times he came home with a nose bleed
Remember his laugh, and the silly jokes he told
Remember the split pants you couldn't sew
I know it's hard
Each parent deals with the loss differently
Together you will find the strength...you will see
Just know that you have the love and support of your friends
It is Jesus who is there to the very End

# *It's Me*

*It's me, I said*
*As I dropped to my knees beside my bed*
*I need to talk to you*
*I don't know what else to do*
*I have tried and failed no fault of my own*
*If I can get pass the mountain, I know it will be gone*
*I know that You are aware and that You do care*
*Of what is going on in my life*
*So Jesus make all that is wrong, right*
*Then I know I will be able to sleep tonight*
*I know we talk often enough*
*Not only when things are rough*
*I try always to say Thank You*
*For all the things that You do*
*My faith and trust is in You*
*Your strength is what sees me through*

# *It's His Love*

*He woke me up this morning*
*I felt alive with the day*
*I picked up my word to hear what he had to say*
*"You have not chosen me, but I have chosen you"*
*I have never known such a special feeling*
*I have come to experience not only His joy*
*But also the power of His healing*
*Throughout my mind, body and soul*
*His love has made me whole*
*What he did was not at a whim*
*He loved me before I ever loved Him*
*He loves me so much you see*
*That He would sacrifice His life for me*

## *Lost In Thoughts*

*When night falls and all its quiet and still*
*I sit and remember just how much God is real*
*I notice the stars and the moon that hang out in space*
*When morning comes night leaves not a trace*
*Not even the creatures that roam at night*
*What comes in the morning is the breaking of light*
*For the moon and the stars are gone from sight*

*There are things in my life that must be done*
*At this moment I won't hurry nor will I run*
*I will take time and remember it all*
*How Winter turns to Spring, then there is Summer then Fall*
*After three months of snow*
*I am glad to see it go*
*For the warmth of the sunshine*
*It gives you such peace of mind*

*Looking out of the window at what I see*
*A squirrel scrambling up a tree*
*The flower that has not yet bloomed*
*I turn to look in my child's room*
*To see her sleeping in her crib*
*With her thumb in her mouth lying perfectly still*
*I silently move from her room*
*For it's time that I leave very soon*
*I can become very wrought*
*When I get lost in my thoughts*

# *Mother's Prayer*

*It's after the baths are done*
*And you are ready to be tucked in for the night*
*Then Mama comes in and turns on the light*
*A Bible story she's already read*
*As she kneels beside you at your bed*
*Mama begins to pray*

*"Lord we thank you for this day, for your protection*
*And for showing us the way. For food, shelter and clothing*
*Lord we thank you"*

*Now it's your turn to pray and in your heart*

*You know what to say*
*"Bless Mama, and Daddy and my sisters and brothers*
*In Jesus' name. Amen"*

*She turns off the light and kisses you good night*
*Feeling very safe you close your eyes*
*Knowing that you are loved*
*You peek out one eye to thank God above*
*For each night you went to bed with Mother's Prayers*
*Always knowing that Mama cares*
*Through times good and bad you were always aware*
*What kept you safe was Mother's Prayers*

***A Tribute to***
***Mother Lillian Dunlap***

# *Oh! Man*

*What has happened to the morals of man*
*Even his values you don't understand*
*His conscience seared*
*There is nothing in life he seems to fear*
*Life is just that*
*Just look at the facts*
*Everyday you read about all sorts of Crimes*
*Boys who are not men but doing hard Time*
*Murders, violence and abortions*
*Business partners who are guilty of extortion*
*Today it seems to be about one's self*
*His accomplishments, his money too*
*It is amazing the things man will do*
*Divorce rates are high*
*The truth believed as a Lie*
*Read your Bible for we are living in the last days*
*It is time for man to change his wicked ways*
*A heart that seems to be one so cold*
*Pray that he has not yet sold his soul*
*Evil intention there seems to be*
*Only God can set his soul free*
***Oh Man!***

# *Silence of the Lamb*
# *(The Lamb of God)*

*Over two thousand years ago*
*The Bible records it so*
*An angel told of the lamb's birth*
*How He would come to the earth*
*Of a virgin, who had found favor*
*She would give birth to our Savior*
*Of a lowly estate he would be born*
*Who knew that one-day*
*His Mother and Followers would mourn*

*Herod tried to find where the lamb laid*
*Thousands still seek him today*
*The Pharisees and Sadducees sought his life*
*They had no idea that Jesus was the Christ*
*He only did good and had such great compassion for man*
*Remember the scars and the nail prints in His hands*
*Jesus was the lamb that was lead to the slaughter*
*He came to redeem your sons and daughters*
*When they came to the Garden to take Him away*
*Not one word did He say*
*He is the Lamb who can take away your sins*
*It was Nicodemus, who asked how to be born again*

*We who are His children testify of Him*
*Therefore others may know*
*He is the only way in which you can go*
*Yes! they hung Him to the cross*
*So that you and I wouldn't be lost*
*Remember how they whipped Him all night long*
*He is the Lion of the Tribe of Judah that sits on the throne*
*The Lamb suffered for you and I*
*That one day we would meet Him in the sky*

# *The Shepherd's Flock*

*He is the Shepherd of a sometimes disobedient flock*
*The things they desire to do has put Him in a state of shock*
*Now these are not all babes in Christ*
*They know what is right*
*Shaking his head at many of them*
*Wishing they would understand they don't do things at a whim*
*Prayer and guidance is what they should seek*
*God's commandments and statutes they need to keep*
*His love for them is very real*
*For the Good Shepherd has placed on them a seal*
*Them that are His another they will not follow*
*His voice only do they obey*
*They won't wander nor will they stray*

*Like the sheep and goats*
*God will do the separating in time*
*So keep this in mind*
*So when He (Jesus) comes you are not left behind*
*The Shepherd sees to His sheep's needs*
*He won't forsake them neither will He leave*
*He (The Pastor) is the watchman over their souls*
*He does what he is told*
*For his instructions are from on High*
*Where we all will see Jesus by and by*
*May he present God a worthy stock*
*The Shepherd of an obedient flock*

# *The Heart Of Man*

*I read an article today*
*Of the pain and suffering of yesterday*
*Oh! It's a time that has gone by*
*But still I ask myself why*
*The Old World as it has been called Nations that rise to power*
*Like Humpty Dumpty they too had a great fall*
*Lives that were lost*
*Death was the alternate cost*
*Some for liberty, justice and all*
*History will recall the greatest to the small*
*I was touched by what I read*
*Of the lives that are now dead*
*Musicians, Poets, Writers and simple people too*
*A heavy price you pay because of everything you lose*
*Socialism in a land were only ONE is right*
*For freedom and justice you must fight*
*As long as I can remember, where there is hatred in the heart of*
*man*
*There have been battles fought in every part of our great land*
*People who buy guns*
*For other's safety is where others run*
*What has happened to the heart of man*
*When he buys a gun, because he knows he can*
*If Man is killed off who then is left to stand*
*There have been wars and yes murders in the street*
*When One person suffers, another can't sleep*
*There has been so much bad news in this Land*
*It will take God only to change the Heart of Man*

# *The Light*

*It was dark and I could not see*
*I was just about at the end of the tunnel*
*I knew God had to be leading me*
*There was a beacon of light*
*I felt a little stronger*
*I didn't have to wait much longer*
*I knew everything would be all right*
*Thank you! Lord for the light*

# *TRAINING OF A CHILD*

FOLLOWING THESE RULES AS A CHILD
Builds character, and maturity
TRAIN UP A CHILD IN THE WAY THAT HE SHOULD GO
There are things he will come to know
IF YOU BEAT THEM THEY WILL NOT DIE
If you are gullible they will tell you a lie
IF YOU SPARE THE ROD YOU WILL SPOIL THE CHILD
Too much freedom, he becomes wild
CHILDREN, HONOR THY MOTHER AND FATHER
To give your child praise or even a hug should not be a
bother
WHEN I WAS A CHILD I ACTED AS A CHILD
If you think that he has forgotten wait awhile
Take them to Sunday school
So they learn the GOLDEN RULE

# *The Quality Of*

*Remember the quality of Life*
*Now! Man will kill at any price*
*Remember the quality of the family*
*Girls now appear to be so manly*
*Just look at the way they dress*
*It makes you wonder, even try to guess*

*Boys who have feminine ways*
*Will tell you they're gay*
*Can we bring back yesterday, I think not*
*Things in the world have changed a whole lot*
*Parents have to work so they are absent from the home*
*Therefore, the children are left all alone*
*The quality of time*
*Who knows what is on a person's mind*
*The structure of the family has changed*
*Not very much remains*

*Romance*
*Take a chance*

# A Husband Loved

*Through your husband's eyes*
*He only spoke the truth and never a lie*
*He said you were his wife all the days of his life*
*You were his friend and companion he could count on*
*The man that you love is now gone*
*So many memories turning in your head*
*Remember the love you shared instead*
*This man who was your husband and your friend*
*The things he did will make you smile again*
*Remember how you laughed and talked*
*It was during many evening walks*
*So many years you were together*
*Through the good times and even the stormy weather*
*There was nothing you didn't share*
*The little things he did that showed he cared*
*He lives in our children this you are aware*
*It's through them that he is always there*
*He was your husband all his life*
*Now he's gone from sight*

# *A Kiss*

*Now when I was little my Daddy used to kiss me*
*On the cheek before going to bed*
*Now I have a husband and he kisses me instead*
*My kids would give me a kiss when we would say good-bye*
*And when they fell and got a boo-boo I would give them*
*A kiss so they wouldn't cry*

## *Dreamer*

*I do a lot of daydreaming*
*My mind sort of wanders out in space*
*When it's reality I don't want to face*
*That's the place where I go to escape*

*Some say I live in a fairytale*
*Others say I am just good at make believe*
*Others say it's myself who I deceive*

*It doesn't matter because it's there I don't have to be me*
*I am many things in my daydreams*
*I have a voice like a canary, boy can I sing*
*I am a real looker too*
*There aren't many things I can't do*
*I am a chef, a nurse, a photographer even a movie star*

*In my daydreams, you can go far*
*It's only when reality sets in*
*That's when the daydreams have to end*

# He's A Smooth Operator

*Oh Yeah! Didn't he have a line or two*
*Did he try it on you*
*I know he's used it many times before*
*Trying to make the big score*

*"Hey you! Come here girl*
*Can I spend some time in your world*
*I want to know what things you like to do*
*I'm serious I really want to get to know you"*

*Now his voice is smooth as velvet and it will touch*
*The very essence of you*
*He's no amateur, he knows what to do*

*"You see, I've been watching you for a long time*
*And girl you boggle my mind*
*Everything about you is put together just right*
*Ain't nothing you got is slighted*
*Your walk, your voice is sexy when you talk*
*I'd like to play in your hair, run my fingers right through there*
*Your nails are always done*
*And the way you smell huh!*
*You are always dressed to kill*
*You independent women are so strong willed*
*I can tell you are special everything about you says it*
*I like a woman that's a sure fit*
*I know that I'm your Mr. Right*
*Cause like you, I'm all that and tight*
*Like me, I see you watching as I leave your sight"*

*Now Girl! Don't fall for any of that*
*He's just another smooth talking Cool Cat*
*He's used those lines before*
*Now don't you think for one moment I didn't find him hard to*
*ignore*

# *In His Eyes*

*My friends tried to tell me it would happen again*
*I would have to be patient and wait until then*
*That love would find its way back to me*
*I could hardly wait and see*

*I did and found love like I never had before*
*There were gifts and chocolates and there was more*
*Moments I spend with you is like a dream come true*
*Loving you is all I want to do*
*I believe that you love me too*

*When I look into your eyes*
*I see them smiling from deep inside*
*The way you feel, you cannot seem to hide*
*I see love every time I look into our eyes*

# I'll Love You Forever

*I was thinking of you today*
*I was haunted by the memories*
*That wouldn't go away*
*We had only kissed but never touched*
*Seems as though that kiss meant very much*
*Then you turned and walked away*
*What was I suppose to do, what could I say*
*Could I ever change your mind*
*I know it would probably be a waste of my time*
*You know I will love you forever*

*Time has passed but this love for you did last*
*I don't understand why you never gave us a chance*
*All I wanted was to be romanced*
*I heard you never married I wonder why*
*All I wanted was to be your girl and you my guy*
*You were my hopes and my dream*
*I finally realized things were not as they seemed*
*My life has changed but one thing has remained the same*
*You know what*
*I'll Love You Forever*

# *I Love Flowers*
# *(Especially the Rose)*

*I love flowers for their beauty*
*Even better than a diamond or a ruby*
*Now jewelry is nice to have, I will agree*
*I just love flowers especially*
*I love the way flowers smell*
*The fact there is a message they tell*
*Oh! There are flowers of many kinds*
*However, the Rose stands out in my mind*
*It represents romance and true love*
*A time past and years God has granted from above*
*I think that the yellow rose is nice, but my favorite is red*
*To me it is a sign that true love is not dead*
*I love flowers for the joy they bring*
*And how they make my heart sing*
*I will accept a single or a dozen of them*
*Doesn't have to be an occasion, bring at a whim*

# *I'm In Love*

*I'm in Love and it feels so good*
*Then of course being in love should*
*You know that tingling feeling you get inside*
*I'm glowing and it shows cause it's not easy to hide*
*I'm in Love and it feels so right*
*It's like the difference in day and night*
*I'm in Love and I'm grinning all the time*
*The reasons being cause I got him on my mind*
*I'm in Love and this isn't spring*
*But that's ok, I love this feeling that it brings*
*I feel free as a bird*
*With its wings spread surveying this New World*
*No longer viewing love through the eyes of a young girl*
*I know that I love you are just words*
*The messages they carry*
*When spoken from the heart*
*Can do some good or do some damage*
*They can also rip you apart*
*I'm in Love and you know it*
*So what if everyone teases you and won't quit*
*They know the score*
*Because they have been in love before*
*I'm in Love and it feels nice*
*With you it is right*

# *Last Chance*

*Girl! You best make up your mind*
*You know you are running out of time*
*It's all up to you*
*So what are you going to do*
*The field isn't wide open*
*So you best choose*
*Before you mess around and lose*
*It will be such a shame*
*If you throw the game*

# *Men Feel It Too*

*Your pain is real*
*Nevertheless, you are hurting still*
*Hide it though you may*
*I really don't know the right words to say*
*Yes in the past, you have had other romances*
*Isn't love all about taking chances*
*Not that I'm insensitive to you*
*How can I help, tell me what can I do*
*It's too soon to try it again*
*When it's right you will know when*
*Give yourself some time*
*To mend, to heal, to be whole*
*You are a man with a good heart and soul*
*Knowing this as you do*
*The right woman is out there for you*
*Yes men hurt and feel pain too*
*Just like women do*

# *Starting Over Again*

*We did discover each other on the phone*
*There was something different in your tone*
*I was listening to every word you said to me*
*It was hard for me to just let things be*

*Living so far apart, the telephone brought us near*
*I think being in a commitment causes you to fear*
*You were afraid to trust your heart*
*Therefore, instead of coming together we were driven apart*
*You thought it better if we were friends*
*I know with us things will never end*
*It was better that way, I heard you say*

*I didn't dial the wrong number*
*Don't tell me you don't remember*
*We talked for a long time*
*We asked if each were fine*
*We gave it the old college try you and I*

*We have done it before*
*Therefore, we will try it once more*
*We won't remember yesterday's pain*
*It won't be the same*
*This time we will be friends*
*For we are starting over again*

# *That Look*

*There's a twinkle in my eye*
*He's the reason why*
*See the smile on my face*
*It's easy to trace*
*You know that look*
*I've seen it on you*
*I've got that same expression too*
*I have been touched by love*
*I thank my God above*
*For life is Oh, so grand*
*When you have the love of a good man*

*So his heart already knows*
*It's visible, he's in love and it shows*
*There's this devilish grin*
*I heard he told everybody I am a Ten*
*There's a twinkle in his eye*
*Yes! I am the reason why*
*He feels that he is one lucky guy*
*That's all it took*
*For I knew **That Look***

# *Wish It Was Me*

*We didn't meet by chance*
*I wasn't looking for romance*
*I remember seeing you with a friend*
*Is this the way true love begins*
*Tell me how can this be*
*Am I really for you and you for me*

*I heard passion could run deep*
*I will admit, when I first saw you*
*I was knocked off my feet*
*How can I make you believe*
*I can be the woman you need*
*I won't hold back, I will help you succeed*
*I will be your anchor and your strength*
*I know in your life, others have came and went*
*I never imagined or did I conceive*
*I just wish you could see*
*How much I wish it was me*

# *Life's Little Proverbs*

- *Life has winners and losers you…decide which one are you?*

- *Me, myself and I: Love them all.*

- *Sometimes you have to praise yourself when no one else does.*

- *Rest, meditate, reflect, then give thanks.*

- *If your shoes are too big, then check the size, you're wearing someone else's.*

- *There are signs that say: Stop, Wrong Way, Yield and U-Turn. The next time be sure which applies to your situation.*

- *For energy, eat. It's Ok, it really is.*

- *It's Ok to say Good Morning, it just might help….*

- *Whoever told you there is a Mr. Right or even a Miss Right… sometimes we are both wrong.*

- *Sometimes life can be bitter and sweet. The next time you drink something sweet read the back of the label.*

- *There is GOD, then there are gods. I prefer the One and Only "Besides Him there is none other."*

- *Now adults don't play silly little games that kids do, or do they?*

- *Love is funny and it also hurts too.*

- *Clouds can be a bumpy ride and I never sat on one.*

*Other Issues*
*Deal with it....*

# Generational Curses

*There was no spell cast*
*Neither was a chant said*
*Magic wasn't even involved*
*Yet a curse exist passed down*
*From one family member to another*
*Even the doctors say it's genetic*
*Dealing with the curse of*
*High blood pressure, heart disease*
*And diabetes*
*A chain that can be broken*
*Changing what happened before*
*One day at a time*

## *Focus*

*Not on what was, or what if*
*The present is now, the past is gone*
*The future is to come*
*Set your sights on what you can*
*Do better today*

# *Identify Me*
# *(This is Who I Am)*

*I am not a "you" girl…I have a name*
*Nor am I a "them"…I'm just one person (singular)*
*Neither am I a "You people"…I do belong to an ethnic group*
*Look at me and see…Yeah! That's right*
*That I am a woman…Independent, self assured beautiful Black*
*woman*
*Not a "y'all"…Tell me what's that*
*I have a name that was given to me…Let me introduce myself*
*If you can, forget my race, creed, or color…Well! Can you*
*Then we are getting somewhere…How about that*

# *If You Could*

*What if all the mistakes you've made, were erased*
*And you could start over again*
*Getting things right the first time around*

*You would watch your weight closely*
*You wouldn't color your hair, yourself*
*You'd buy less on credit. Pay cash for more*
*The things you would do right first time around*

*The house you bought that had so many problems*
*Such as the leaky faucet in the shower, the crack in the chimney*
*The car, the dealership said was a steal*
*If only it was the first time around*

*The implants you now discovered weren't worth*
*The money, the pain or trouble*
*The affair you had, that broke up a family*
*The things you would do right the first time around*

*That big wedding you couldn't really afford*
*Or the one you needed to tell how you felt*
*But you let him get away*
*Or choosing the right mate*
*Something you said, you now regret*
*But it was too late to take it back*
*Things you would do right the first time around*

# *Just Between Us*

*Girl! You can tell me your secret*
*You know I won't tell nobody else*
*I know how to keep things to myself*
*Not one word will I reveal*
*Cause I'm telling you my lips are sealed*

*What! Huh, no kidding she did what?*
*Did you see it?*
*For real, girl huh, huh*
*You must be joking*
*I really can't believe it*

*I smile as she left my side*
*Wait until Bess hears this*
*She will have a fit*
*Come to think of it, I wouldn't have said a thing*
*Some things should be kept to oneself*
*Never tell something you don't want told*
*Now that saying is very old*

# *A Young Soldier*

*Why is it boys who are not yet men?*
*Go into battle green?*
*Inexperienced to what is going to happen*
*In their lives and to their life*
*What of the uncertainty of it all*
*Can he kill another person?*
*Once was faceless now has a face*
*Will he be able to conger up the courage?*
*That is somewhere deep inside of him*
*To do what is required of a solider?*
*It's kill or be killed*
*He knows the training he's had*
*Now faced with the reality of War*
*He won't be a boy, he'll be a man*

# *What A Change*

*Looking back over time you realize*
*The signs of age, caught you unaware*
*Nothing is what is used to be*
*No longer that teenager any more*
*The high energy has now downloaded*
*There are wrinkles, once smooth skin*
*The figure once admired by many is gone*
*The long beautiful black hair, hints of gray*

*There are dreams yet unfulfilled*
*Promises you made to yourself not kept*
*Everything happened so quickly for time*
*Kept on going while you procrastinated*
*Another birthday has come and gone*
*Leaving memories of shoulda, coulda*
*But didn't, now there are regrets*

*Enjoy the new woman you have become*
*Self assured, re-established and independent*
*Not afraid to take chances with whatever comes*
*Even having a little fun, trying new things*
*It's that what change is all about*

# *Your Word*

*Is a promise made*
*It's a guarantee to something*
*A vow spoken*
*Your commitment to perform*
*Bonding you together*
*For deals were made and sealed*
*On your word*

# *I'm Sorry*

*Your car stopped, but I can't help you*
*I don't know your name?*
*So your house was broken into*
*I didn't know; I didn't see a thing*
*You asked if I could identify the murderer*
*I can't get involved*
*Who did you think I was?*
*A Good Samaritan*
*Have you forgotten the day and time?*
*In which we live, be for real*
*I can't take that chance*
*What can I say, I'm sorry*

## *My Muse, My Teacher*

*So! I came in thinking I was ahead of the game*
*Boy was I wrong*
*What I've learned, I am grateful*
*So I like rhyme*
*Everybody doesn't, but that's Ok*
*Look at me, I found out I could*
*Write without it*
*I discovered another endless flow*
*You became someone new to me*
*Yeah! The Muse*
*The thoughts are still there*
*But different*
*It still flows*
*Just a little different from before*
*In my very first book now published*
*Is what you inspired*
*Other Issues*
*The very first one was*
*I'm Sorry then came*
*Focus, followed by Generational Curses*
*If I Could, and Identify Me*
*And many others*
*So Teacher the Muse*
*Thank you for unlocking*
*Another door for me*
*My Muse*

# *The Pain Of It All*

*Beneath the layer of skin*
*Beyond the tissue and the fat*
*Surrounded by my ribs*
*Is the largest muscle*
*Called the heart*

*There's another rhythm*
*Out of sync with what is regular*
*Only the pain of it is excruciating*
*Unlike anything I have felt before*

*It's hard to identify*
*It is affecting my breathing*
*I am afraid*
*What's going on?*
*Is it stress?*
*Is it a heart attack?*

*O Lord, no*
*I would have felt the pain moving up my arm*
*Ok! I said, calm down*

*Don't start playing doctor*
*It's painful, I told the medic*
*As he began to examine me*
*It's only a muscle spasm*
*Was his reply*
*Glad to hear that*
*With medication, I would be all right*

*So beneath the layer of skin*
*Beyond the tissue and the fat*
*Surrounded by my ribs*
*Is my heart*
*That continues to beat*

Genie was born in Fayetteville, North Carolina to Elder Ernest G. Simmons and Carnell Cousar Simmons. She is a graduate of E.E. Smith Senior High School. She is the divorced mother of four children, Levi Jr., Gregory, Roslyn and Jennifer Tyler.

She graduated from Mott Community College in Flint, Michigan where she received an Associate Degree in Culinary Arts and Food Service Management. She has received many certificates of class completions one being from Metro Chamber of Commerce in Flint, Michigan for Entrepreneur Training.

Genie's talents include songwriting, singing, photography and sewing. She has written several unpublished novels as well as plays. She enjoys traveling also. Genie loves the Lord and credits Jesus for the talents He has given her.

CPSIA information can be obtained at www.ICGtesting.com
Printed in the USA
BVOW07s2123041113

335451BV00001B/5/P